Laudatio!

Two Toccatas for Organ

Table of Contents

Grimoaldo Macchia

Dedicated to Samuel Metzger, Organist and Music Associate at Second Presbyterian Church, Memphis, Tennessee

Toccata on Amazing Grace

Sw. Trumpet en Chamade (opt. Reeds 8', 4')
Gt. Full to Mixtures (no Reeds)
Ch. Full to Mixtures (no Reeds)
Ped. Full 16', 8', 4', Gt. to Ped.

Grimoaldo Macchia
based on an early
American melody

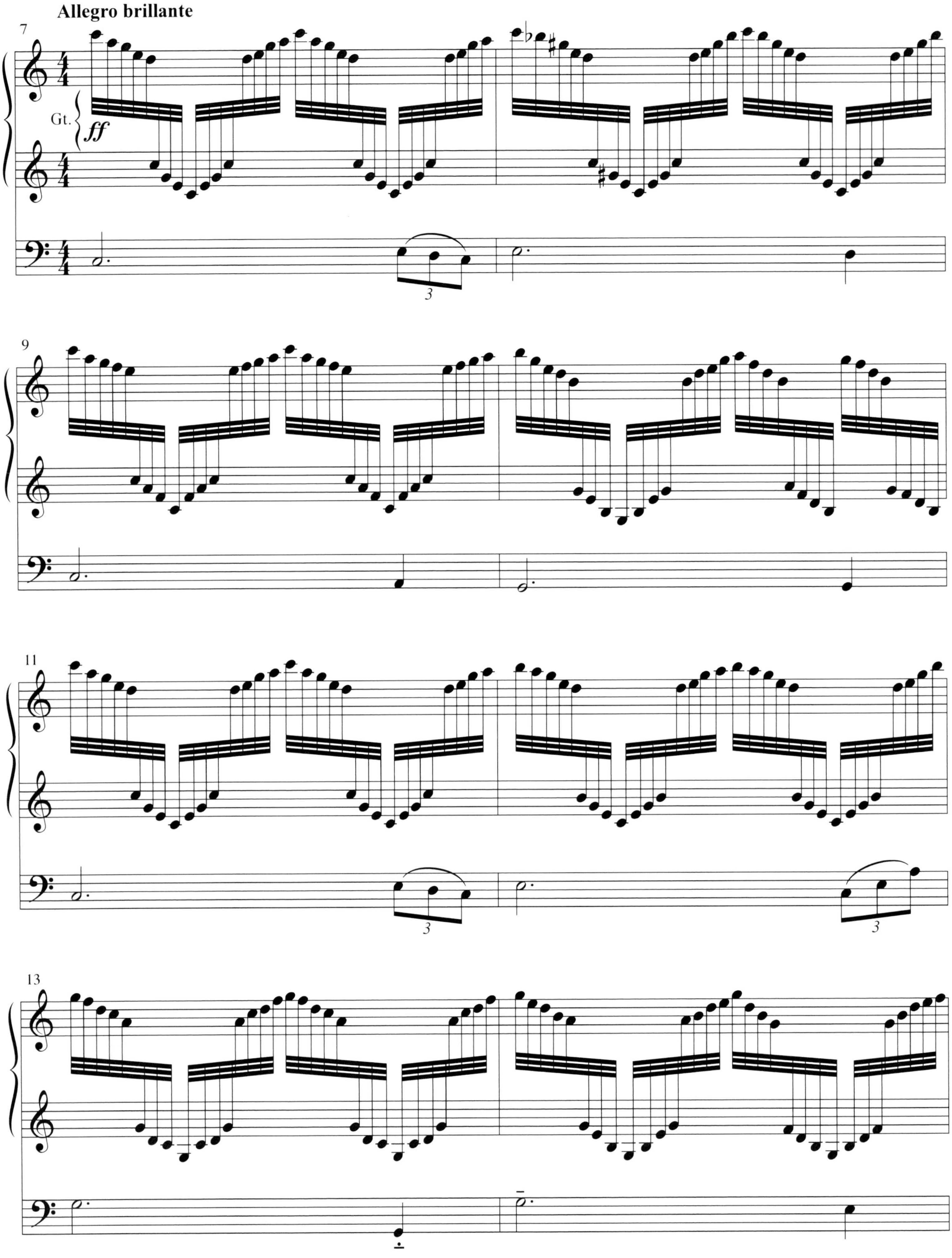
Allegro brillante
7
Gt.
ff
9
11
13

15
17
19
21
gliss.

23
Festoso
Sw.
ff
-Sw. to Ped.
ff
Moderato e giocoso
26
Ch.
f
Sw. opt.
change to Solo Tuba
ff
28
30

32
34
36
38

40
42
Maestoso e solenne
Gt.
fff
Sw.
Gt.
fff
45
Sw.
Gt.
48
Sw.
Gt.

51
54
57
Sw.
fff
ffff

to Harry L. Huff, Minister of Music and Organist, Old South Church, Boston

Toccata on the Bells of Westminster

Grimoaldo Macchia

Sw. Full, Mixtures (no Reeds), 4' coupler
Gt. Full, Mixtures, Reeds, 4' coupler
Ch. Full, Mixtures (no Reeds)
Ped. Full 16', 8', 4', Gt. to Ped., Sw. to Ped.

Allegro

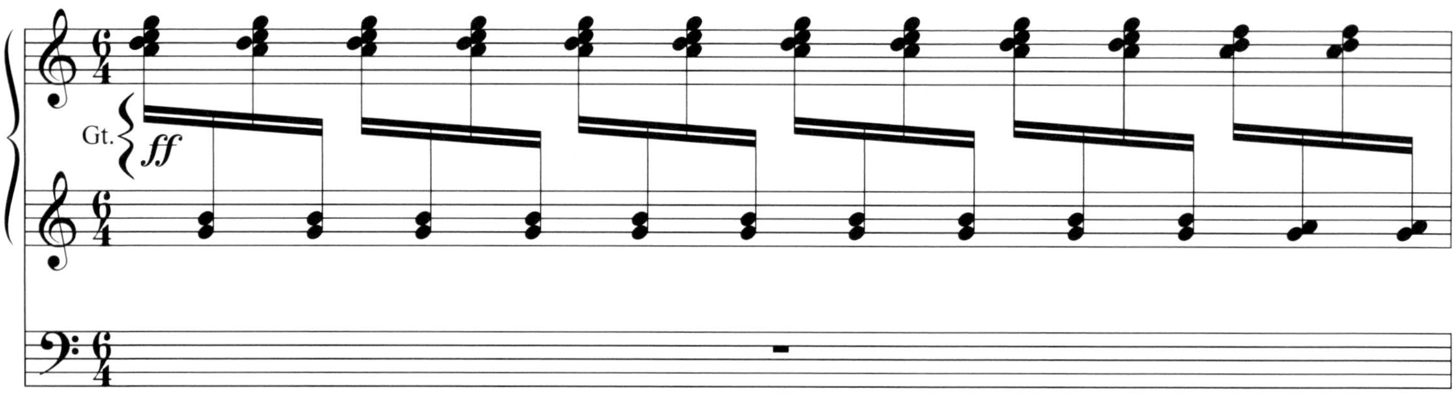

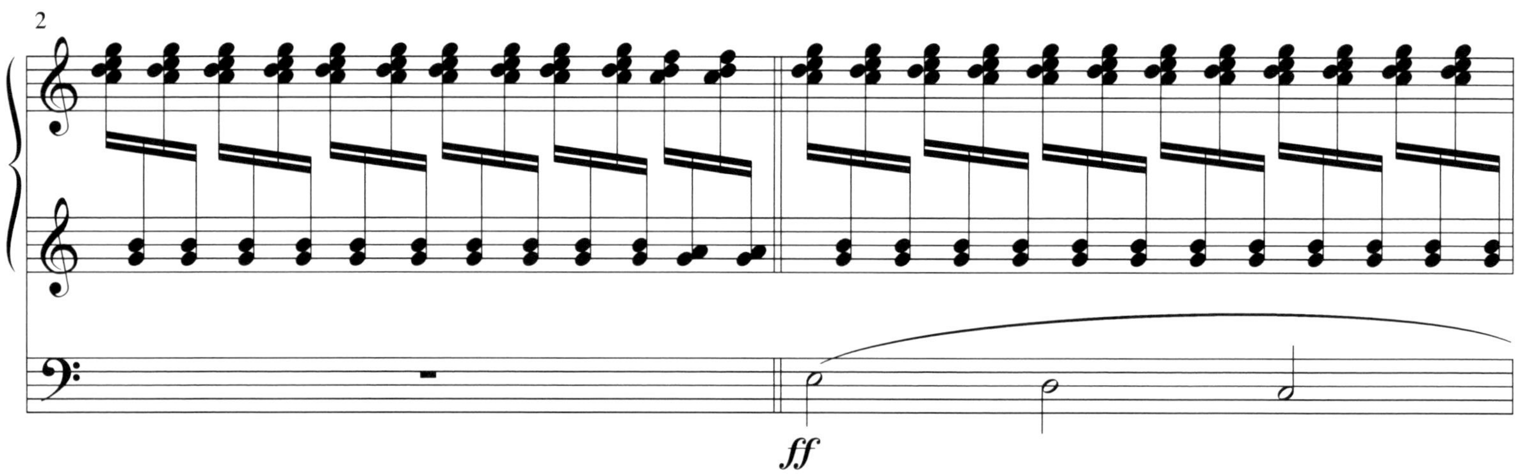

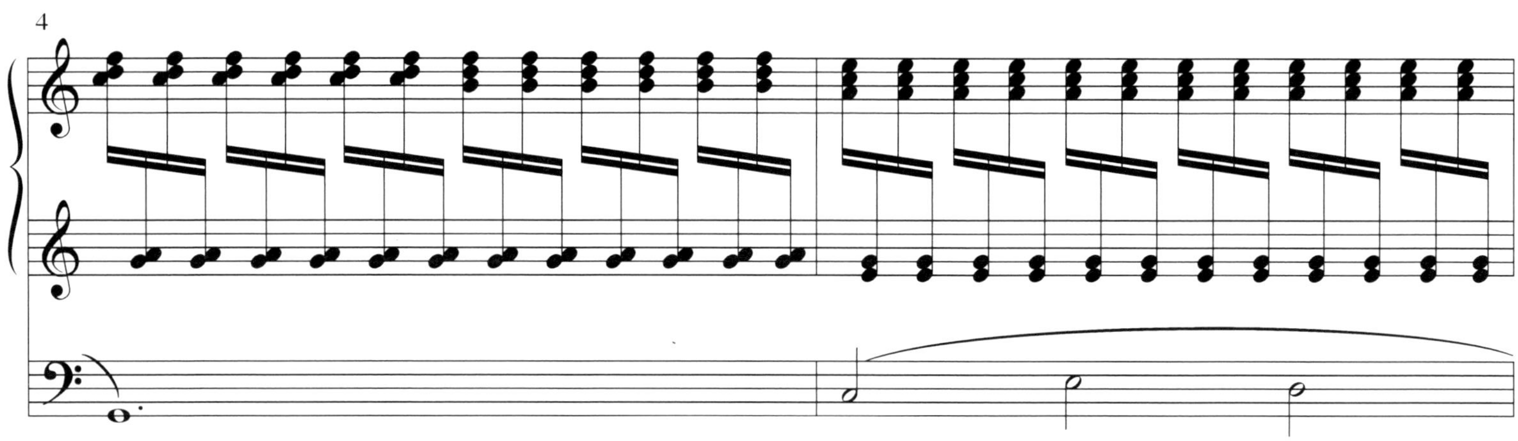

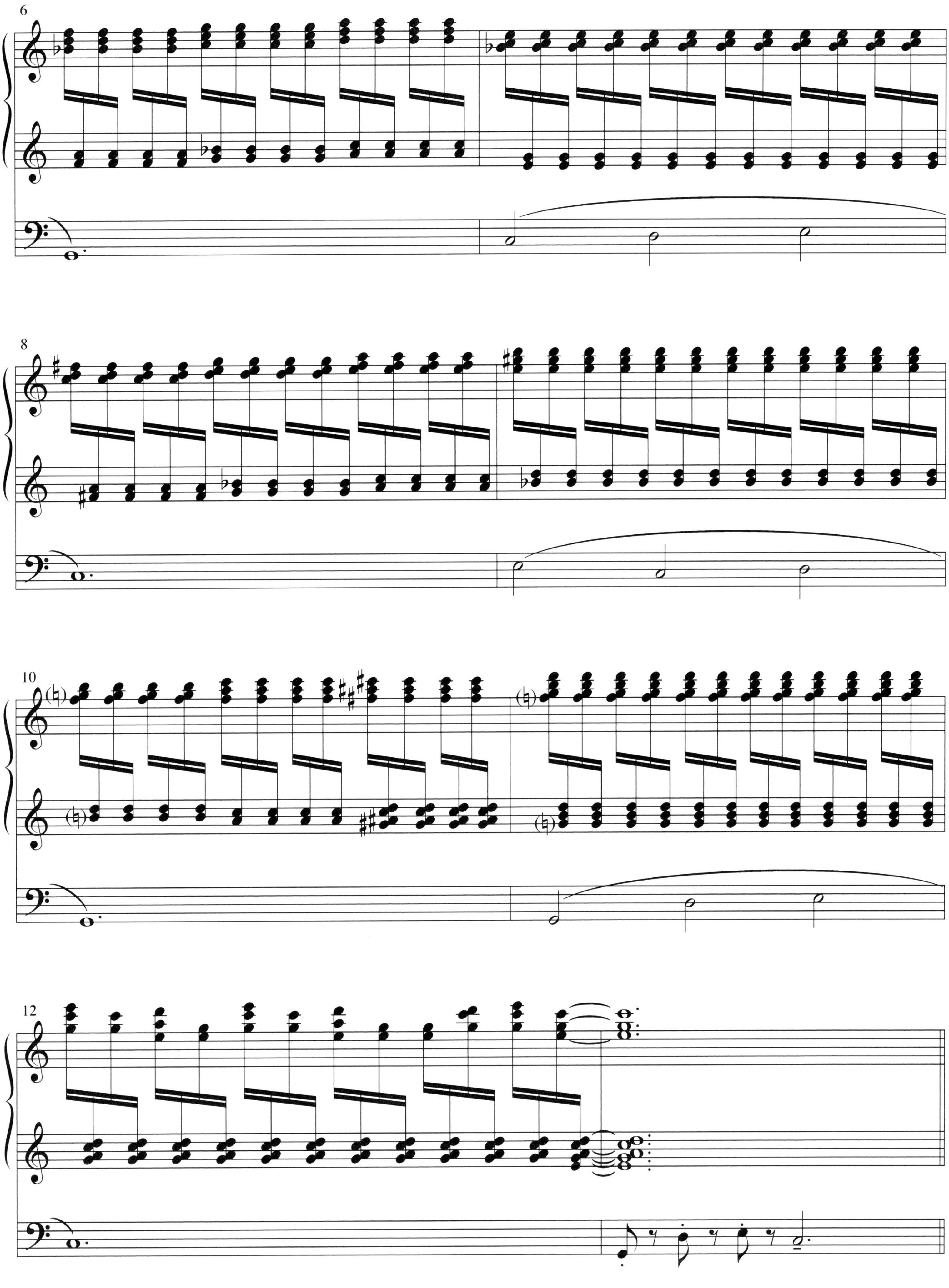

Sw.
Ch.
legato
8va

22
24
Sw. Reeds
Ch.
Sw. Reeds
26
Ch.
Sw. Reeds
Ch.
Sw. Reeds
28
Gt. Tuba or Reeds
3

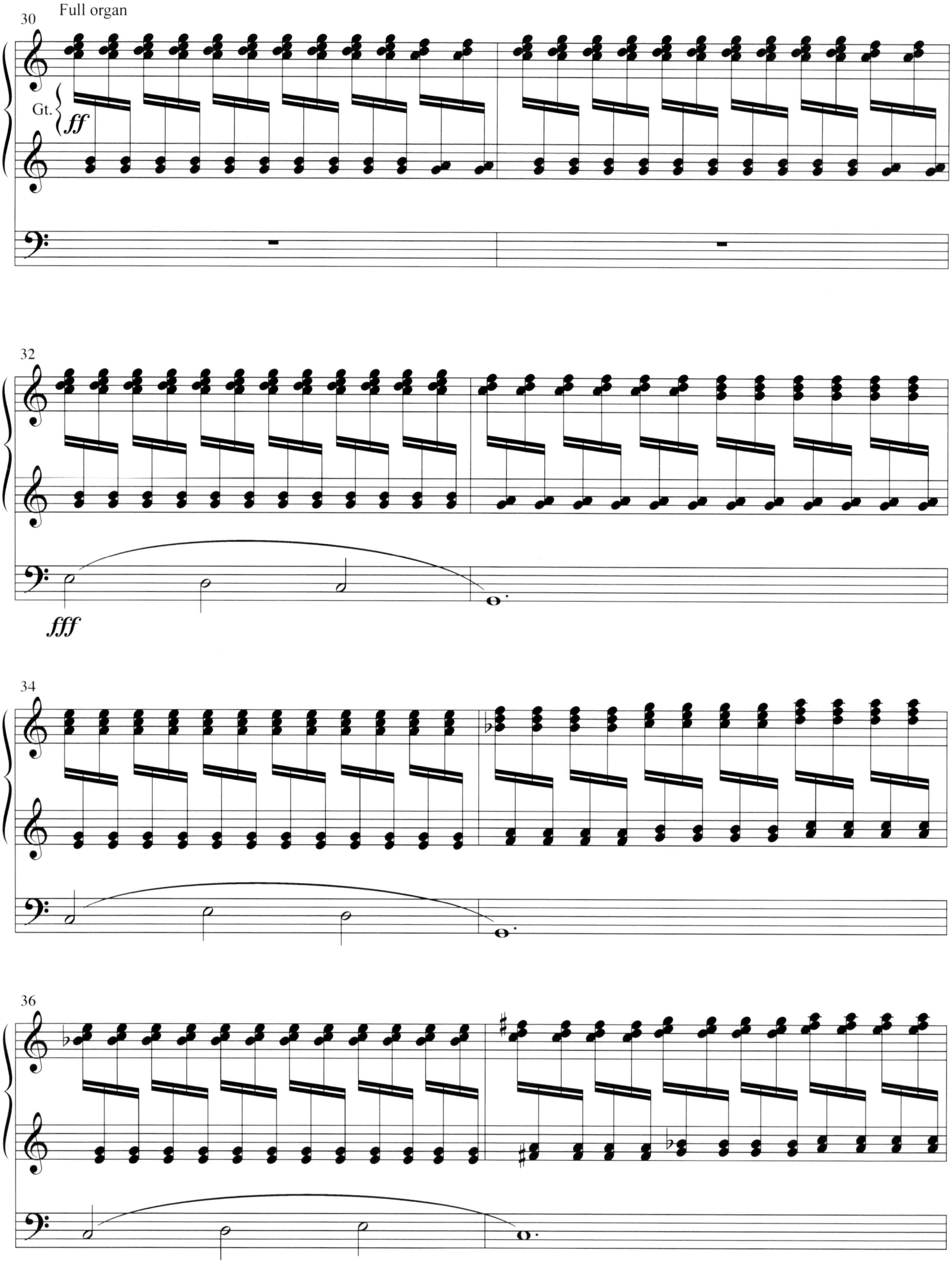
30
Full organ
Gt.
ff
32
fff
34
36

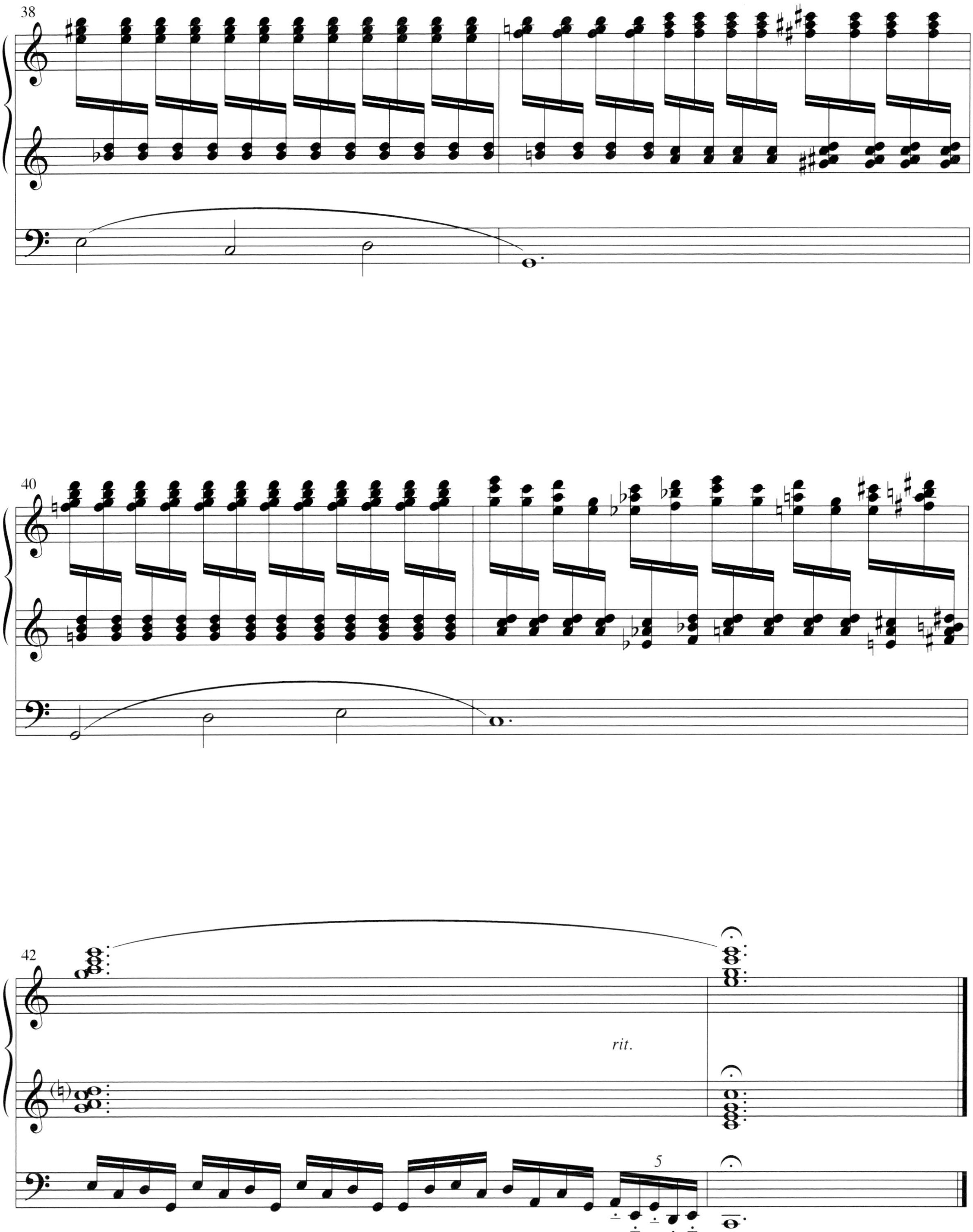
38
40
42
rit.
5
ffff

Laudatio!

Two Toccatas for Organ

Grimoaldo Macchia